EVERYMAN,
I WILL GO WITH THEE
AND BE THY GUIDE,
IN THY MOST NEED
TO GO BY THY SIDE

EVERYMAN'S LIBRARY
POCKET POETS

LULLABIES
AND
POEMS FOR
CHILDREN

SELECTED AND
EDITED BY
DIANA SECKER LARSON

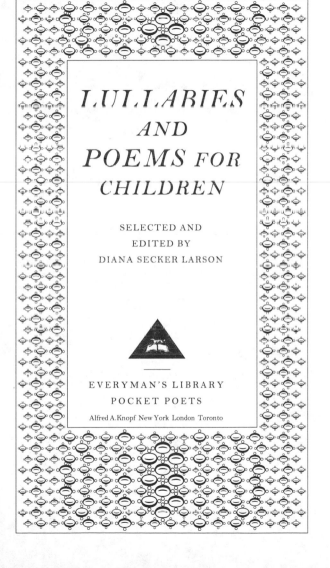

EVERYMAN'S LIBRARY
POCKET POETS

Alfred A. Knopf New York London Toronto

THIS IS A BORZOI BOOK
PUBLISHED BY ALFRED A. KNOPF

This selection by Diana Secker Larson first published in
Everyman's Library, 2002
Copyright © 2002 by Everyman's Library

Third printing (US)

A list of acknowledgments to copyright owners appears at the back
of this volume.

US website: www.randomhouse.com/everymans

ISBN 0-375-41419-3 (US)
1-84159-748-1 (UK)

A CIP catalogue record for this book is available from the British Library

Typography by Peter B. Willberg

Typeset in the UK by AccComputing, North Barrow, Somerset

Printed and bound in Germany by GGP Media GmbH, Pössneck

CONTENTS

NIGHT FALLS

SPELLS AND CHARMS

8

9

POEMS FOR CHILDREN

NONSENSE

10

SILLY STORIES

FANTASIES

FOREWORD

"Music hath charms to soothe the savage breast." This, surely, is the hope embodied in the age-old custom of singing infants to sleep. There is something half wild about the little creature in the crib, with its fierce hunger and its primitive rage, wailing at us from the far side of the language divide. And there is something charmlike in the power of rhythm, rhyme, and song to lure the young listener across that divide.

Lullabies are the first poems most children hear, even before they know what words mean. We croon toora-looras and hush-a-byes, trusting to the musicality of language to bring peace, calm, and delight to our restless young. The poems we call lullabies serve a range of incantatory purposes, from the most basic – to soothe into silence or sleep – to the more ambitious – to bless and protect from harm and even to express hopes for the future when, in the words of Gershwin's "Summertime," our children will "spread [their] wings and take the sky."

This collection intersperses lullabies drawn from the rich oral traditions of the world with poems and lyrics by famous authors. A wide variety of literary and musical greats have tried their hand at the humble lullaby, from Mozart and Brahms to Shakespeare, Tennyson, and Kipling. Alongside these classics are

13

poems to infants written by such modern poets as Sylvia Plath, Thom Gunn, and Donald Justice, whose more sophisticated "lullabies" will strike a chord with the adult reader. For the slightly older child who has already begun to spread his or her linguistic wings, the final section contains an array of poems to enchant and amuse, from the simplest nursery rhymes to the witty absurdities of Lewis Carroll, T. S. Eliot, and Ogden Nash. Old favorites and new surprises await you in this collection, whether you use them to lull children to sleep or to awaken them to the world of poetry.

DIANA SECKER LARSON

LULLABIES

HUSH LITTLE BABY

GOLDEN SLUMBERS

Golden slumbers kiss your eyes,
Smiles awake you when you rise.
Sleep, pretty wantons, do not cry,
And I will sing a lullaby:
Rock them, rock them, lullaby.

Care is heavy, therefore sleep you;
You are care, and care must keep you.
Sleep, pretty wantons, do not cry,
And I will sing a lullaby:
Rock them, rock them, lullaby.

SLEEP, LITTLE ONE

Sleep, little one, go to sleep.
So peaceful the birds and the sheep,
Quiet are meadow and trees,
Even the buzz of the bees,
The silvery moonbeams so bright,
Down through the window give light,
O'er you the moonbeams will creep,
Sleep, little one, go to sleep.
Good night, good night.

CRADLE SONG

What does little birdie say
In her nest at peep of day?
Let me fly, says little birdie,
Mother, let me fly away.
Birdie, rest a little longer,
Till the little wings are stronger;
So she rests a little longer,
Then she flies away.

What does little baby say,
In her bed at peep of day?
Baby says, like little birdie,
Let me rise and fly away.
Baby, sleep a little longer,
Till the little limbs are stronger;
If she sleeps a little longer,
Baby too shall fly away.

ALFRED, LORD TENNYSON (1809–92)   21

LULLABY, OH, LULLABY

Lullaby, oh, lullaby!
Flowers are closed and lambs are sleeping;
 Lullaby, oh, lullaby!
Stars are up, the moon is peeping;
 Lullaby, oh, lullaby!
While the birds are silence keeping,
 (Lullaby, oh, lullaby!)
Sleep, my baby, fall a-sleeping,
 Lullaby, oh, lullaby!

LIE A-BED

Lie a-bed,
Sleepy head,
Shut up eyes, bo-peep;
Till daybreak
Never wake·—
Baby, sleep.

OH HUSH THEE, MY DOVE

Oh hush thee, my dove,
Oh hush thee, my rowan,
Oh hush thee, my lapwing,
My little brown bird.

Oh hush thee, my dove,
Oh hush thee, my rowan,
Oh hush thee, my lapwing,
My little brown bird.

Oh, fold thy wing and seek thy nest now,
Oh, shine the berry on the bright tree.
The bird is home from the mountain and valley,
Oh hush thee, my birdie, my pretty dearie.

SLEEP, BABY, SLEEP

Sleep, baby, sleep,
Our cottage vale is deep;
The little lamb is on the green,
With woolly fleece so soft and clean –
Sleep, baby, sleep.

Sleep, baby, sleep,
Down where the woodbines creep;
Be always like the lamb so mild,
A kind, and sweet, and gentle child –
Sleep, baby, sleep.

TRADITIONAL

TOORA, LOORA, LOORA

Toora, loora, loora,
Oh, toora, looralie,
Toora, loora, loora,
Hush now, don't you cry.

Toora, loora, loora,
Oh, toora, looralie,
Toora, loora, loora,
That's an Irish lullaby.

SLEEP, BABY SLEEP

Sleep, baby sleep,
Thy father tends his sheep,
Thy mother shakes the dreamland tree,
Down falls a little dream for thee.
Sleep, baby sleep.

Sleep, baby sleep,
The large stars are the sheep,
The little stars are lambs I guess,
The golden moon the shepherdess,
Sleep, baby sleep.

Sleep, baby sleep,
Away and tend thy sheep,
Away thou black dog fierce and wild,
And do not harm my little child.
Sleep, baby sleep.

TRADITIONAL GERMAN   27

SLUMBER TIME IS DRAWING NEAR

Slumber time is drawing near,
Night is gath'ring round us.
Stars will all be bright and clear,
When the sandman has found us.
Dream sweet dreams the long night through,
Mother will be near to you.
Go to sleep my dear one.

SLEEP MY BABY

Sleep my baby near to me,
Lu lu lu, lu lu lu,
Close your velvet eyes.
Far away in their nest
Baby birds flutter down to rest.
High in the trees, far from harm,
Tiny monkey sleeps
Deep in his mother's arms.

TRADITIONAL NIGERIAN

ROCKABY BABY

Rockaby baby, o go to sleep now, o go to sleep now,
My little Jesus wants to go to sleep, God bless him,
    God bless him.

Little flowing fountain, sparkling and musical,
Nightingale of the woods crying as you sing,
Hush while the cradle's swaying, swaying and
    swinging,
Rockaby little baby, rockaby, go to sleep.
My little flower, like the roses, like the gilliflowers,
What are you dreaming of that makes you smile so
    sweetly?

Little flowing fountain, sparkling and musical,
Nightingale of the woods crying as you sing,
What dream you of my baby, tell me my soul?
What dream you of my baby, tell me my soul?

Birds, fountains, winds and breezes, o let him sleep
    now, o let him sleep now,
Let him go on dreaming, dreaming and smiling.

SEÑORA SANTA ANA

Señora Santa Ana,
   why does the baby cry?
Oh, for an apple he has lost.
Señora Santa Ana,
   why does the baby cry?
Oh, for an apple he has lost.

Hush little baby, sleep now I pray.
Here comes an old man to take you away.

BYE-O, BYE-O, BYE-O BABY

Bye-o, bye-o, bye-o baby,
Close your little baby eyes.
You are mommy's little baby,
You are daddy's little prize.

HUSH, MY LITTLE BIRD

Hush, my little bird, close your drowsy eyes,
    Ey-loo-loo-loo.
Rest in peace my child, under starry skies,
    Ey-loo-loo-loo.
Mother's always near, so you need not fear,
    Ey-loo-loo-loo.
Sleep and have sweet dreams, while your young life
      seems, full of light and love,
    Ey-loo loo-loo.

TRADITIONAL   33

WATCHING
OVER ME

LULLY, LULLA

Lully, lulla, thou little tiny child,
By by, lully lullay.

O sisters too,
How may we do
For to preserve this day
This poor youngling,
For whom we do sing,
By by, lully lullay?

Herod, the king,
In his raging,
Charged he hath this day
His men of might,
In his own sight,
All young children to slay.

That woe is me,
Poor child for thee!
And ever morn and day,
For thy parting
Neither say nor sing
By by, lully lullay!

Lully, lulla, thou little tiny child,
By by, lully lullay.

ANONYMOUS, 15TH CENTURY   37

A ROCKING HYMN

Sweet baby, sleep: what ails my dear?
    What ails my darling thus to cry?
Be still, my child, and lend thine ear,
    To hear me sing thy lullaby.
My pretty lamb, forbear to weep;
Be still, my dear; sweet baby, sleep.

Thou blessèd soul, what can'st thou fear,
    What thing to thee can mischief do?
Thy God is now thy father dear,
    His holy Spouse thy mother too.
Sweet baby, then, forbear to weep;
Be still, my babe; sweet baby, sleep.

Whilst thus thy lullaby I sing,
    For thee great blessings ripening be;
Thine Eldest Brother is a king,
    And hath a kingdom bought for thee.
Sweet baby, then, forbear to weep;
Be still, my babe; sweet baby, sleep.

Sweet baby, sleep, and nothing fear;
  For whosoever thee offends
By thy protector threatened are,
  And God and angels are thy friends.
Sweet baby, then, forbear to weep;
Be still, my babe, sweet baby, sleep.

CRADLE HYMN

Hush! my dear, lie still and slumber,
    Holy angels guard thy bed!
Heavenly blessings without number
    Gently falling on thy head.

Sleep, my babe; thy food and raiment,
    House and home, thy friends provide;
All without thy care or payment,
    All thy wants are well supplied.

How much better thou'rt attended
    Than the Son of God could be,
When from heaven He descended,
    And became a child like thee!

Soft and easy is thy cradle:
    Coarse and hard thy Saviour lay,
When His birthplace was a stable,
    And His softest bed was hay.

Was there nothing but a manger
    Cursèd sinners could afford
To receive the heavenly stranger?
    Did they thus affront their Lord?

See the kinder shepherds round Him,
  Telling wonders from the sky;
Where they sought Him, there they found Him,
  With His Virgin mother by.

See the lovely babe a-dressing,
  Lovely infant, how He smiled!
When He wept, the mother's blessing
  Soothed and hushed the holy child.

Lo, He slumbers in His manger,
  Where the hornèd oxen fed;
Peace, my darling; here's no danger,
  Here's no ox a-near thy bed.

May'st thou live to know and fear Him,
  Trust and love Him all thy days;
Then go dwell for ever near Him,
  See His face, and sing His praise!

BRAHMS'S LULLABY

Lullaby and good night,
  With roses bedight,
With lilies o'erspread
  Is baby's wee bed.
Lay thee down now and rest,
  May thy slumber be blest.
Lay thee down now and rest,
  May thy slumber be blest.

Lullaby and good night,
  In the soft evening light,
Like a rose in its bed,
  Lay down your sweet head.
When morning is near,
  I will wake you, my dear.
When morning is near,
  I will wake you, my dear.

Lullaby and good night,
  You're your mother's delight.
Shining angels beside
  My darling abide.
Soft and warm is your bed,
  Close your eyes and rest your head.
Soft and warm is your bed,
  Close your eyes and rest your head.

Sleepyhead, close your eyes,
    Mother's right here beside you.
I'll protect you from harm,
    You will wake in my arms.
Guardian angels are near,
    So sleep on, with no fear.
Guardian angels are near,
    So sleep on, with no fear.

Lullaby, and sleep tight
    Hush! My darling is sleeping,
On his sheets white as cream,
    With his head full of dreams.
When the sky's bright with dawn,
    He will wake in the morning.
When noontide warms the world,
    He will frolic in the sun.

JOHANNES BRAHMS (1833—97)   43
LYRICS BY FRITZ SIMROCK

ALL THROUGH THE NIGHT

Sleep, my child, and peace attend thee,
    All through the night;
Guardian angels God will send thee,
    All through the night;
Soft the drowsy hours are creeping,
Hill and vale in slumber sleeping,
I my loving vigil keeping,
    All through the night.

While the moon her watch is keeping,
    All through the night;
While the weary world is sleeping,
    All through the night;
O'er thy spirit gently stealing,
Visions of delight revealing,
Breathes a pure and holy feeling,
    All through the night.

Hark, a solemn bell is ringing,
    Clear through the night;
You, my love, are heav'nward winging,
    Home through the night.
Earthly dust from off thee shaken,
By good angels art thou taken;
Soul immortal shalt thou waken,
    Home through the night.

44   SIR HAROLD BOULTON (1859–1935)

WHEN AT NIGHT I GO TO SLEEP
From *Hansel and Gretel*

When at night I go to sleep,
Fourteen angels watch do keep;
Two my head are guarding,
Two my feet are guiding,
Two are on my right hand,
Two are on my left hand,
Two who warmly cover,
Two who o'er me hover,
Two to whom 'tis given
To guide my steps to heaven.

MATTHEW, MARK, LUKE, AND JOHN

Matthew, Mark, Luke, and John,
Bless the bed that I lie on.
Four corners to my bed,
Four angels round my head;
One to watch and one to pray,
And two to guide me through the day.

ANGELS WATCHING OVER ME

All night, all day,
Angels watching over me, my Lord.
All night, all day,
Angels watching over me.

Sun is a-setting in the West;
Angels watching over me, my Lord.
Sleep my child, take your rest;
Angels watching over me.

All night, all day,
Angels watching over me, my Lord.
All night, all day,
Angels watching over me.

When at night I go to sleep,
Angels watching over me, my Lord,
Pray the Lord my soul to keep,
Angels watching over me.

SWING LOW, SWEET CHARIOT

Swing low, sweet chariot,
Comin' for to carry me home,
Swing low, sweet chariot,
Comin' for to carry me home.

I looked over Jordan and what did I see,
Comin' for to carry me home,
A band of angels comin' after me,
Comin' for to carry me home.

If you get to heaven before I do,
Comin' for to carry me home,
Tell all my friends I'm comin' there, too,
Comin' for to carry me home.

Swing low, sweet chariot,
Comin' for to carry me home,
Swing low, sweet chariot,
Comin' for to carry me home.

KUMBAYAH

Kumbayah, my Lord, Kumbayah,
Kumbayah, my Lord, Kumbayah,
Kumbayah, my Lord, Kumbayah,
Oh, Lord, Kumbayah.

Someone's crying, Lord, Kumbayah,
Someone's crying, Lord, Kumbayah,
Someone's crying, Lord, Kumbayah,
Oh, Lord, Kumbayah.

Someone's singing, Lord, Kumbayah,
Someone's singing, Lord, Kumbayah,
Someone's singing, Lord, Kumbayah,
Oh, Lord, Kumbayah.

Someone's sleeping, Lord, Kumbayah,
Someone's sleeping, Lord, Kumbayah,
Someone's sleeping, Lord, Kumbayah,
Oh, Lord, Kumbayah.

Kumbayah, my Lord, Kumbayah,
Kumbayah, my Lord, Kumbayah,
Kumbayah, my Lord, Kumbayah,
Oh, Lord, Kumbayah.

TRADITIONAL WEST INDIAN

THE VOYAGE
OF SLEEP

WYNKEN, BLYNKEN, AND NOD
(DUTCH LULLABY)

Wynken, Blynken, and Nod one night
   Sailed off in a wooden shoe
Sailed on a river of crystal light,
   Into a sea of dew.
"Where are you going, and what do you wish?"
   The old moon asked the three.
"We have come to fish for the herring fish
   That live in this beautiful sea;
   Nets of silver and gold have we!"
        Said Wynken,
        Blynken,
        And Nod.

The old moon laughed and sang a song,
   As they rocked in the wooden shoe,
And the wind that sped them all night long
   Ruffled the waves of dew.
The little stars were the herring fish
   That lived in that beautiful sea –
"Now cast your nets wherever you wish –
   Never afeard are we";
   So cried the stars to the fishermen three:
        Wynken,
        Blynken,
        And Nod.

All night long their nets they threw
    To the stars in the twinkling foam –
Then down from the skies came the wooden shoe,
    Bringing the fishermen home;
'Twas all so pretty a sail it seemed
    As if it could not be,
And some folks thought 'twas a dream they'd dreamed
    Of sailing that beautiful sea –
    But I shall name you the fishermen three:
            Wynken,
            Blynken,
            And Nod.

Wynken and Blynken are two little eyes,
    And Nod is a little head,
And the wooden shoe that sailed the skies
    Is a wee one's trundle-bed.
So shut your eyes while mother sings
    Of wonderful sights that be,
And you shall see the beautiful things
    As you rock in the misty sea,
    Where the old shoe rocked the fishermen three:
            Wynken,
            Blynken,
            And Nod.

MY BED IS A BOAT

My bed is like a little boat;
    Nurse helps me in when I embark;
She girds me in my sailor's coat
    And starts me in the dark.

At night, I go on board and say
    Good-night to all my friends on shore;
I shut my eyes and sail away
    And see and hear no more.

And sometimes things to bed I take,
    As prudent sailors have to do;
Perhaps a slice of wedding-cake,
    Perhaps a toy or two

All night across the dark we steer:
    But when the day returns at last,
Safe in my room, beside the pier,
    I find my vessel fast.

THE WHITE SEAL'S LULLABY

Oh! hush thee, my baby, the night is behind us,
    And black are the waters that sparkled so green.
The moon, o'er the combers, looks downward to find us
    At rest in the hollows that rustle between.
Where billow meets billow, there soft be thy pillow;
    Ah, weary wee flipperling, curl at thy ease!
The storm shall not wake thee, nor shark overtake thee,
    Asleep in the arms of the slow-swinging seas.

BABY'S BED'S A SILVER MOON

Baby's bed's a silver moon,
Sailing o'er the sky,
Sailing o'er the sea of sleep,
While the stars float by.

Sail, baby, sail,
Far across the sea,
Only don't forget to come
Back again to me.

Baby's fishing for a dream,
Fishing near and far,
Her line a silver moonbeam is,
Her bait a silver star.

Sail, baby, sail,
Far across the sea,
Only don't forget to come
Back again to me.

57

THE LAND OF NOD

From breakfast on all through the day
At home among my friends I stay;
But every night I go abroad
Afar into the land of Nod.

All by myself I have to go,
With none to tell me what to do –
All alone beside the streams
And up the mountain-sides of dreams.

The strangest things are there for me,
Both things to eat and things to see,
And many frightening sights abroad
Till morning in the land of Nod.

Try as I like to find the way,
I never can get back by day,
Nor can remember plain and clear
The curious music that I hear.

PROMISES

LULLABY OF AN INFANT CHIEF

O hush thee, my baby, thy sire was a knight,
Thy mother a lady, both lovely and bright;
The woods and the glens, from the towers which we see,
They all are belonging, dear baby, to thee.

O fear not the bugle, though loudly it blows,
It calls but the warders that guard thy repose;
Their bows would be bended, their blades would be red,
Ere the step of a foeman drew near to thy bed.

O hush thee, my baby, the time soon will come,
When thy sleep shall be broken by trumpet and drum;
Then hush thee, my darling, take rest while you may,
For strife comes with manhood, and waking with day.

SIR WALTER SCOTT (1771–1832)   61

ROCK-A-BYE, BABY

Rock-a-bye, baby,
On the treetop,
When the wind blows
The cradle will rock;
When the bough breaks
The cradle will fall,
And down will come baby,
Cradle and all.

Rock-a-bye, baby,
Your cradle is green,
Father's a King
And Mother's a Queen.
Sister's a Lady
And wears a gold ring,
Brother's a drummer
And plays for the king.

Rock-a-bye, baby,
Way up on high,
Never mind baby,
Mother is nigh.
Up to the ceiling,
Down to the ground,
Rock-a-bye, baby,
Up hill and down.

ALL THE PRETTY LITTLE HORSES

Hush-a-bye, don't you cry,
Go to sleep little baby.
When you wake you shall have
All the pretty little horses.
Blacks and bays, dapples and grays,
Coach and six white horses.
Hush-a-bye, don't you cry,
Go to sleep little baby.

CHERRIES ARE RIPE

Cherries are ripe, cherries are ripe,
And Barbara shall have some.
Robin wants no cherry pie,
Quick he eats and away he'll fly;
But my little child, so gentle and mild,
She (He) surely shall have some pie.

BAIOUSHKI BAIOU

Go to sleep my darling baby,
Baioushki baiou.
See the moon is shining on you,
Baioushki baiou.

I will tell you many stories
If you close your eyes.
Go to sleep my darling baby,
Baioushki baiou.

ROZENKES MIT MANDLEN
(RAISINS AND ALMONDS)

To my little one's cradle in the night,
Comes a new little goat snowy white.
That goat will trot to the market,
While mother her watch will keep,
To bring back raisins and almonds.
Sleep, my little one sleep.

YORUBA LULLABY

Be quiet child, and do not cry.
I shall bring you a big toad
From our farm in Awututu.
Be quiet child, and do not cry.

O SWEETLY DOES MY BABY SLEEP

O sweetly does my baby sleep;
When he awakes from slumber deep,
Bright sparkling jewels I'll show him,
Gay coloured balls I'll throw him.

My baby in his cradle lies,
To him I sing sweet lullabies,
Gently his cradle I'm rocking,
Whilst o'er him I am watching.

O Virgin Mary, Mother of Christ,
Pour blessings on this babe of mine;
Fill his arms full of posies,
Sweet smelling herbs and roses.

FAIS DODO (GO TO SLEEP)

Go to sleep, my sweet little brother,
Go to sleep, and you'll have a treat.
Mama makes a cake, it's ready to bake;
Papa's down below and he's making cocoa.
Go to sleep, my sweet little brother,
Go to sleep, my sweet little one.

LITTLE BABY SWEETLY SLEEP

Little baby sweetly sleep, do not stir,
I will give a coat of fur.
I will rock you, rock you, rock you,
I will rock you, rock you, rock you.
See the coat to keep you warm,
Gently round your little form.

YOUR BROTHER HAS A FALCON

Your brother has a falcon,
    Your sister has a flower;
But what is left for mannikin,
    Born within an hour?

I'll nurse you on my knee, my knee,
    My own little son;
I'll rock you, rock you, in my arms,
    My least little one.

ARMENIAN LULLABY

If thou wilt shut thy drowsy eyes,
    My mulberry one, my golden sun!
The rose shall sing thee lullabies,
    My pretty cosset lambkin!
And thou shalt swing in an almond-tree,
With a flood of moonbeams rocking thee –
A silver boat in a golden sea,
    My velvet love, my nestling dove,
        My own pomegranate blossom!

The stork shall guard thee passing well
    All night, my sweet! my dimple-feet!
And bring thee myrrh and asphodel,
    My gentle rain-of-springtime!
And for thy slumbrous play shall twine
The diamond stars with an emerald vine
To trail in the waves of ruby wine,
    My myrtle bloom, my heart's perfume,
        My little chirping sparrow!

And when the morn wakes up to see
    My apple bright, my soul's delight!
The partridge shall come calling thee,
    My jar of milk-and-honey!
Yes, thou shalt know what mystery lies
In the amethyst deep of the curtained skies,
If thou wilt fold thy onyx eyes,
    You wakeful one, you naughty son,
      You cooing little turtle!

SUMMERTIME

Summertime an' the livin' is easy,
Fish are jumpin', an' the cotton is high.
Oh, yo' daddy's rich, an yo' ma is good-lookin',
So hush, little baby, don' you cry.

One of these mornin's you goin' to rise up singin',
Then you'll spread yo' wings an' you'll take the sky.
But till that mornin' there's a nothin' can harm you
With Daddy an' Mammy standin' by.

POEM FOR A BIRTHDAY

I give you my **H**eart
   the size of a fist
I give you an **A**pple
   red as the world
I give you a **P**orpoise
   for how high it leaps
I give you a **P**earl
   moon from the deep
I give you **Y**arrow
   starry sun-ray
I give you **B**eauty
   brazen and furled
I give you an **I**ris
   spare indigo
I give you **R**ome
   not built in a day
I give you a **T**roika
   to come and go
I give you my **H**and
   a matter of course
I give you **D**esire
   the rainbow's end
I give you **A**stonishment's
   bountiful stores
I give you **Y**ears
   right round the bend

CYNTHIA ZARIN (1959–)   75

NIGHT FALLS

From NIGHT

The sun descending in the west,
The evening star does shine;
The birds are silent in their nest,
And I must seek for mine.
The moon, like a flower
In heaven's high bower,
With silent delight
Sits and smiles on the night.

WILLIAM BLAKE (1757–1827)

TWINKLE, TWINKLE, LITTLE STAR

Twinkle, twinkle, little star,
How I wonder what you are!
Up above the world so high,
Like a diamond in the sky.
Twinkle, twinkle, little star,
How I wonder what you are!

When the blazing sun is gone,
When he nothing shines upon,
Then you show your little light,
Twinkle, twinkle, all the night.
Twinkle, twinkle, little star,
How I wonder what you are!

Then the trav'ler in the dark
Thanks you for your tiny spark.
He could not see which way to go,
If you did not twinkle so.
Twinkle, twinkle, little star,
How I wonder what you are!

In the dark blue sky you keep,
Often through my curtains peep.
For you never shut your eye,
'Til the sun is in the sky.
Twinkle, twinkle, little star,
How I wonder what you are!

DAY IS DONE

Day is done,
Gone the sun,
From the lake,
From the hills,
From the sky.
All is well,
Safely rest.
God is nigh.

THE COTTAGER TO HER INFANT

The days are cold, the nights are long,
The north wind sings a doleful song;
Then hush again upon my breast;
All merry things are now at rest,
   Save thee, my pretty love!

The kitten sleeps upon the hearth,
The crickets long have ceased their mirth;
There's nothing stirring in the house
Save one wee, hungry, nibbling mouse,
   Then why so busy thou?

Nay! start not at that sparkling light;
'Tis but the moon that shines so bright
On the window-pane bedropped with rain:
Then, little darling, sleep again,
   And wake when it is day!

DOROTHY WORDSWORTH (1771–1855)   83

NOW THE DAY IS OVER

Now the day is over,
   Night is drawing nigh,
Shadows of the evening
   Steal across the sky.

Now the darkness gathers,
   Stars begin to peep,
Birds and beasts and flowers
   Soon will be asleep.

Jesu, give the weary
   Calm and sweet repose;
With thy tenderest blessing
   May our eyelids close.

Grant to little children
   Visions bright of thee;
Guard the sailors tossing
   On the deep blue sea.

Comfort every sufferer
   Watching late in pain;
Those who plan some evil
   From their sin restrain.

Through the long night-watches
    May thine angels spread
Their white wings above me,
    Watching round my bed.

When the morning wakens,
    Then may I arise
Pure and fresh and sinless
    In thy holy eyes.

Glory to the Father,
    Glory to the Son,
And to thee, blest Spirit,
    Whilst all ages run.

AUTUMN LULLABY

The sun has gone from the shining skies,
    Bye, baby, bye,
The dandelions have closed their eyes,
    Bye, baby, bye.
The stars are lighting their lamps to see
If babes and squirrels and birds and bees
Are sound asleep as they should be,
    Bye, baby, bye.

The squirrel keeps warm in his furs of gray,
    Bye, baby, bye,
'Neath feathers, birdies are tucked away,
    Bye, baby, bye.
In yellow jackets, the bees sleep tight
And cuddle close through the chilly night,
My baby's snug in her gown of white,
    Bye, baby, bye.

The squirrel nests in a big oak tree,
    Bye, baby, bye.
He finds a hole in the trunk, you see,
    Bye, baby, bye.
The robin's home is a nest o'erhead,
The bees, they nest in a hive instead,
My baby's nest is her little bed,
    Bye, baby, bye.

THE EVENING IS COMING

The evening is coming, the sun sinks to rest,
The crows are all flying straight home to the nest.
"Caw," says the crow as he flies overhead,
It's time little people were going to bed.

The flowers are closing, the daisy's asleep,
The primrose is buried in slumber so deep,
Closed for the night are the roses so red,
It's time little people were going to bed.

The butterfly, drowsy, has folded its wing,
The bees are returning, no more the birds sing,
Their labor is over, their nestlings are fed,
It's time little people were going to bed.

Goodnight, little people, goodnight and goodnight,
Sweet dreams to your eyelids 'til dawning of light,
The evening has come, there's no more to be said,
It's time little people were going to bed.

LITTLE RED BIRD

Little red bird of the lonely moor,
Lonely moor, lonely moor,
Little red bird of the lonely moor,
O where did you sleep in the night?

Out on a gorse bush dark and wide,
Dark and wide, dark and wide,
Swift rain was falling on every side,
O hard was my sleep last night.

Did I not sleep on the swaying briar,
Swaying briar, swaying briar,
Tossing about as the wind rose higher,
O little I slept last night!

Did I not sleep on the cold wave's crest,
Cold wave's crest, cold wave's crest,
Where many a man has taken his rest,
And O! my sleep was too light.

Wrapped in two leaves I lay at ease,
Lay at ease, lay at ease,
As sleeps the young babe on its mother's knees.
O sweet was my sleep last night!

Little red bird of the lonely moor,
Lonely moor, lonely moor,
Little red bird of the lonely moor,
O where did you sleep in the night?

TRADITIONAL MANX   89
TRANSLATED BY MONA DOUGLAS

NOW SLEEP LITTLE BABY

Now sleep little baby, don't cry little darling,
The angels are coming with shadows of evening.
The rays of the moonlight spin fine threads of silver,
To shine on my baby, asleep in his cradle.
The rays of the sun, the blue of the sky,
Will wake him from dreams when morning is nigh.
Now sleep little baby, with eyes bright as diamonds,
And brilliant as starlight that shines from the heavens.

SPELLS AND
CHARMS

THE FAIRIES SING TITANIA
TO SLEEP
From *A Midsummer Night's Dream*, II ii

You spotted snakes with double tongue,
   Thorny hedgehogs, be not seen;
Newts and blind-worms, do no wrong,
   Come not near our fairy queen.

    Philomel, with melody,
    Sing in our sweet lullaby.
Lulla, lulla, lullaby, lulla, lulla, lullaby:
      Never harm,
      Nor spell, nor charm:
      Come our lovely lady nigh;
      So, good night, with lullaby.

Weaving spiders, come not here;
   Hence, you long-legg'd spinners, hence!
Beetles black, approach not near;
   Worm nor snail, do no offence.

    Philomel, with melody,
    Sing in our sweet lullaby.
Lulla, lulla, lullaby, lulla, lulla, lullaby:
      Never harm,
      Nor spell, nor charm:
      Come our lovely lady nigh;
      So, good night, with lullaby.

WILLIAM SHAKESPEARE (1564–1616)   93

ARIEL'S SONG
From *The Tempest*, I ii

Come unto these yellow sands,
    And then take hands:
Curtsied when you have, and kiss'd, –
    The wild waves whist, –
Foot it featly here and there;
And, sweet sprites, the burden bear,
    Hark, hark!
    Bow, wow,
    The watch-dogs bark:
    Bow, wow,
    Hark, hark! I hear
The strain of strutting Chanticleer
    Cry, cock-a-diddle-dow.

THE SANDMAN

The flowers are sleeping
Beneath the moon's soft light,
With heads close together
They dream through the night.
And leafy trees rock to and fro
And whisper low –
Sleep, sleep, lullaby,
Oh sleep, my darling child.

Now birds that sang sweetly,
To greet the morning sun,
In little nests are sleeping
Now twilight has begun.
The cricket chirps its sleepy song,
Its dreamy song –
Sleep, sleep, lullaby,
Oh sleep, my darling child.

The Sandman comes on tiptoe
And through the window peeps,
To see if little children
Are in their beds asleep.
And when a little child he finds
Casts sand in his eyes –
Sleep, sleep, lullaby,
Oh sleep, my darling child.

JOHANNES BRAHMS (1833–97)   95

MONDAY'S CHILD

Monday's child is fair of face;
Tuesday's child is full of grace;
Wednesday's child is full of woe;
Thursday's child has far to go;
Friday's child is loving and giving;
Saturday's child works hard for a living;
The child that is born on the Sabbath day,
Is bonny, and blithe, and good, and gay.

BED IS TOO SMALL

Bed is too small for my tiredness;
Give me a hillside with trees.
Tuck a cloud up under my chin.
Lord, blow the moon out, please.

Tuck me to sleep in a little of the arms,
Sing me a lullaby of dreams.
Tuck a cloud up under my chin.
Lord, blow the moon out, please.

TRADITIONAL

HUSH-A-BYE MY BABY

Hush-a-bye my baby,
   hush-a-bye my sun;
Hush-a-bye, part of my heart.

St Anne and St Joachim,
   make up the cradle
In a bed of lemon balm.

And for a pillow,
   put a jasmine plant,
So the baby will sleep
   like an angel.

AGAINST DARK'S HARM

The baby at my breast
suckles me to rest.
Who lately rode my blood
finds me further flood,
pulls me to his dim
unimagined dream.

Amulet and charm
against dark's harm,
coiled in my side,
shelter me from fright
and the edged knife,
despair, distress
and all self-sickness.

ANNE HALLEY (1928–   )   99

STORIES IN
SONG

MARY'S LAMB

Mary had a little lamb,
   Its fleece was white as snow,
And everywhere that Mary went
   The lamb was sure to go;
He followed her to school one day –
   That was against the rule,
It made the children laugh and play
   To see a lamb at school.

And so the teacher turned him out,
   But still he lingered near,
And waited patiently about,
   Till Mary did appear.
And then he ran to her and laid
   His head upon her arm,
As if he said, "I'm not afraid –
   You'll shield me from all harm."

"What makes the lamb love Mary so?"
   The little children cry;
"Oh, Mary loves the lamb, you know,"
   The teacher did reply,
"And you each gentle animal
   In confidence may bind,
And make it follow at your call,
   If you are always kind."

SARAH JOSEPHA HALE (1788–1879)   103

MINNIE AND WINNIE

Minnie and Winnie
    Slept in a shell.
Sleep, little ladies!
    And they slept well.

Pink was the shell within,
    Silver without;
Sounds of the great sea
    Wandered about.

Sleep, little ladies,
    Wake not soon!
Echo on echo
    Dies to the moon.

Two bright stars
    Peeped into the shell.
"What are they dreaming of?
    Who can tell?"

Started a green linnet
    Out of the croft;
Wake, little ladies,
    The sun is aloft!

LITTLE BOY BLUE

Little Boy Blue, come blow your horn,
The sheep's in the meadow, the cow's in the corn.
Where is the boy who looks after the sheep?
He's under the haystack, fast asleep.
Will you wake him? No, not I,
For if I do he'll be sure to cry.

OH, MOTHER, HOW PRETTY
THE MOON IS TONIGHT

Oh, mother, how pretty the moon is tonight,
'Twas never so pretty before.
Its two little horns are so sharp and so bright,
I hope they don't grow anymore.

If I were up there with you and my friends,
We'd rock in it nicely you'd see.
We'd sit in the middle and we'd hold by both ends,
Oh, what a nice cradle 'twould be.

I GAVE MY LOVE A CHERRY

I gave my love a cherry without a stone;
I gave my love a chicken without a bone;
I gave my love a ring, without an end;
I gave my love a baby with no cryin'.

How can there be a cherry without a stone?
How can there be a chicken without a bone?
How can there be a ring without an end?
How can there be a baby with no cryin'?

A cherry when it's blooming, it has no stone;
A chicken when it's peeping, it has no bone;
A ring when it's rolling, it has no end;
A baby, when he's sleeping, there's no cryin'.

LAVENDER'S BLUE

Lavender's blue, dilly dilly,
    Lavender's green,
When you are King, dilly dilly,
    I shall be Queen.

Who told you so, dilly dilly,
    Who told you so?
'Twas my own heart, dilly dilly,
    That told me so.

Call up your friends, dilly dilly,
    Set them to work,
Some to the plough, dilly dilly,
    Some to the fork.

Some to the hay, dilly, dilly,
    Some to thresh corn,
Whilst you and I, dilly dilly,
    Keep ourselves warm.

Lavender's blue, dilly dilly,
    Lavender's green,
When you are King, dilly dilly,
    I shall be Queen.

Who told you so, dilly dilly,
    Who told you so?
'Twas my own heart, dilly dilly,
    That told me so.

TRADITIONAL ENGLISH

ORANGES AND LEMONS

Oranges and lemons,
Say the bells of St Clement's.

You owe me five farthings,
Say the bells of St Martin's.

When will you pay me?
Say the bells of Old Bailey.

When I grow rich,
Say the bells of Shoreditch.

When will that be?
Say the bells of Stepney.

I'm sure I don't know,
Says the great bell of Bow.

SHADY GROVE, MY LITTLE LOVE

Shady grove, my little love;
    shady grove I know,
Shady grove, my little love;
    bound for the shady grove.

Peaches in the summertime,
    apples in the fall,
If I can't have the one that I want,
    I won't have none at all.

Fly away my blue-eyed friend,
    fly away my daisy,
Fly away my blue-eyed friend,
    You nearly drive me crazy.

Wish I had a banjo strong,
    strung with golden twine,
And every time I'd pluck on it,
    I'd wish that girl were mine.

Shady grove, my little love;
    shady grove I know,
Shady grove, my little love;
    bound for the shady grove.

TRADITIONAL   111

THE CAMBRIC SHIRT

Can you make me a cambric shirt,
    Parsley, sage, rosemary and thyme,
Without any seam or needle work?
    And you shall be a true lover of mine.

Can you wash it in yonder well,
    Parsley, sage, rosemary and thyme,
Where never sprung water, nor rain ever fell?
    And you shall be a true lover of mine.

Can you dry it on yonder thorn,
    Parsley, sage, rosemary and thyme,
Which never bore blossom since Adam was born?
    And you shall be a true lover of mine.

Now you have ask'd me questions three,
    Parsley, sage, rosemary and thyme,
I hope you'll answer as many for me,
    And you shall be a true lover of mine.

Can you find me an acre of land,
    Parsley, sage, rosemary and thyme,
Between the salt water and sea sand?
    And you shall be a true lover of mine.

Can you plow it with a ram's horn,
    Parsley, sage, rosemary and thyme,
And sow it all over with one pepper corn?
    And you shall be a true lover of mine.

Can you reap it with a sickle of leather,
    Parsley, sage, rosemary and thyme,
And bind it up with a peacock's feather?
    And you shall be a true lover of mine.

When you have done and finish'd your work,
    Parsley, sage, rosemary and thyme,
Then come to me for your cambric shirt,
    And you shall be a true lover of mine.

TRADITIONAL ENGLISH   113

THE SKYE BOAT SONG

Speed bonnie boat like a bird on the wing,
  "Onward," the sailors cry.
Carry the lad that's born to be king
  Over the sea to Skye.

Loud the winds howl, loud the waves roar,
  Thunderclaps rend the air.
Baffled, our foes stand by the shore,
  Follow they will not dare.

Many's the lad fought on that day,
  Well the claymore did wield,
When the night came, silently lay
  Dead on Culloden field.

Though the waves leap, soft will ye sleep,
  Ocean's a royal bed.
Rocked in the deep, Flora will keep
  Watch by your weary head.

Burned are our homes, exile and death
 Scatter the loyal men.
Yet e'er the sword cool in the sheath
 Charlie will come again.

Speed bonnie boat like a bird on the wing
 "Onward," the sailors cry.
Carry the lad that's born to be king
 Over the sea to Skye.

OH, MY DARLING CLEMENTINE

In a cavern in a canyon, excavating for a mine,
Dwelt a miner, forty-niner, and his daughter,
     Clementine.
Oh, my darling, oh, my darling, oh, my darling Clementine,
You are lost and gone forever, dreadful sorry, Clementine.

Light she was and like a fairy, and her shoes were
     number nine,
Herring boxes without topses, sandals were for
     Clementine.

Drove her ducklings to the water, every morning
     just at nine,
Hit her foot against a splinter, fell into the foaming
     brine.

Ruby lips above the water, blowing bubbles soft
     and fine,
Alas, for me! I was no swimmer, so I lost my
     Clementine.

In a churchyard, near the canyon, where the myrtle
     doth entwine,
There grow roses and other posies fertilized by
     Clementine.

Then the miner, forty-niner, soon began to droop
and pine,
Thought he ought to join his daughter, now he's
with his Clementine.

In my dreams, she still doth haunt me, robed in
garments soaked in brine,
Though in life I used to kiss her, now she's dead
I draw the line.
Oh, my darling, oh, my darling, oh my darling Clementine,
You are lost and gone forever, dreadful sorry, Clementine.

THE BIG ROCK CANDY MOUNTAINS

One evening as the sun went down
And the jungle fire was burning,
Down the track came a hobo hiking.
And he said, "Boys I'm not turning,
I'm headed for a land that's far away,
Beside the crystal fountains,
So come with me, we'll go and see
The Big Rock Candy Mountains."

In the Big Rock Candy Mountains,
There's land that's fair and bright,
Where the handouts grow on bushes,
And you sleep out every night.
Where the boxcars are all empty,
And the sun shines every day
On the birds and the bees,
And the cigarette trees,
And the lemonade springs
Where the bluebird sings
In the Big Rock Candy Mountains.

IN MOTHER'S ARMS

THE BABY'S DANCE

Dance, little baby, dance up high,
Never mind baby, mother is by;
Crow and caper, caper and crow,
There little baby, there you go:
Up to the ceiling, down to the ground,
Backwards and forwards, round and round.
Then dance, little baby, and mother shall sing,
With the merry gay coral, ding, ding, a-ding, ding.

ANN TAYLOR (1782–1866)

MOTHER AND CHILD

See where the road bends,
A tiny house stands at the end.
Crooked walls and windows small,
Doors that hardly close at all.
Dog he barks, bad little thing,
In the eaves the swallows sing.
And the sunshine will not last,
For the sun is setting fast.

In the rosy evening sun
Mother sits, the charming one.
Apple red her cheeks must be,
And her son is on her knee.
He is strong as if he grew
Like red rosy apples too.
Spanks his hands in joyful game
'Til he cries "again, again."

There stands cat with arched back
Troubled by a stinging gnat,
Boldly hits it with his paw,
Then stands stately as before.
Mother pats her baby's cheek,
See how soon he falls asleep?
Dreams of angels in the skies
As within his crib he lies.

CRYING, MY LITTLE ONE

Crying, my little one, footsore and weary?
    Fall asleep, pretty one, warm on my shoulder:
I must tramp on through the winter night dreary,
    While the snow falls on me colder and colder.

You are my one, and I have not another;
    Sleep soft, my darling, my trouble and treasure;
Sleep warm and soft in the arms of your mother,
    Dreaming of pretty things, dreaming of pleasure.

MOTHER'S SONG

There's not a rose where'er I seek
   As comely as my baby's cheek.
There's not a comb of honey-bee,
   So full of sweets as babe to me.
And it's O! sweet, sweet! and a lullaby.

There's not a star that shines on high,
   Is brighter than my baby's eye.
There's not a boat upon the sea,
   Can dance as baby does to me.
And it's O! sweet, sweet! and a lullaby.

No silk was ever spun so fine
   As is the hair of baby mine.
My baby smells more sweet to me
   Than smells in spring the elder tree.
And it's O! sweet, sweet! and a lullaby.

MAMMY, MAMMY TOLD ME-O

Mammy, mammy told me-o,
I'm the sweetest little baby in the country-o.
I looked in the glass and found it so,
Just as mammy told me-o.

WAY UP HIGH IN THE CHERRY TREE

Way up high in the cherry tree,
If you look, you will see,
Mother Robin and babies three,
High, high in the tree.
See the nest in the treetops,
Swinging, swaying.

Mother Robin is singing,
Singing her babies to sleep.
Way up high in the cherry tree,
If you look, you will see,
Mother Robin and babies three,
High, high in the tree.

I'VE FOUND MY BONNY BABE A NEST

I've found my bonny babe a nest,
On slumber tree,
I'll rock you here to rosy rest,
Astore Machree.
Oh lulla lo sing all the leaves,
On slumber tree,
Till everything that hurts or grieves,
Afar must flee.

THE GARTAN MOTHER'S LULLABY

Sleep, O babe, for the red bee hums the silent
    twilight's fall,
Aoibheall from the grey rock comes, to wrap the
    world in thrall.
A leanbhan O, my child, my joy, my love, my
    heart's desire,
The crickets sing you lullaby, beside the dying fire.

Dusk is drawn, and the green man's thorn is
    wreathed in rings of fog,
Siabhra sails his boat till morn, upon the starry
    bog.
A leanbhan O, the paly moon hath brimmed her
    cusp in dew,
And weeps to hear the sad sleep tune, I sing
    O love to you.

Faintly sweet doth the chapel bell, ring o'er the
    valley dim,
Tearmann's peasant voices swell, in fragrant
    evening hymn.
A leanbhan O, the low bell rings, my little lamb
    to rest,
And angel-dreams till morning sings, its music
    in your breast.

JOSEPH CAMPBELL (1879–1944)

CAN YE SEW CUSHIONS?

O can ye sew cushions, and can ye sew sheets?
And can ye sing ba-lu-lo when the bairn greets?
And hie and baw birdie, and hie and baw lamb,
And hie and baw birdie my bonnie wee lamb.

Hee-o-wee-o, what will I do wi' ye?
Black's the life that I lead wi' you.
Many o' you, little for to gi'e you,
Hee-o-wee-o, what will I do wi' you?

I've placed my cradle, on yon holly top,
And aye as the wind blows my cradle will rock.
O hush-a ba baby, o ba-lily-loo,
And hee and ba birdie my bonnie wee doo.

Hee-o-wee-o, what will I do wi' ye?
Black's the life that I lead wi' you.
Many o' you, little for to gi'e you,
Hee-o-wee-o, what will I do wi' you?

SUO-GÂN

Sleep my baby on my bosom,
Closely nestle safe and warm;
Mother wakeful, watches o'er you,
Round you folded mother's arm.
Sweet there's nothing near can hurt you,
Nothing threatens here your rest;
Sleep my baby, sleep and fear not,
Sleep you sweetly on my breast.

Lulla lulla sweetly slumber,
Mother's treasure, slumber deep;
Lulla, lulla, now you're smiling,
Smiling, dear one, through your sleep.
Say are angels bending o'er you
Smiling down from heaven above?
Is that heavenly smile your answer?
Love from dreamland answering love?

Hush my treasure, 'tis a leaflet
Beating, beating, on the door;
Hush my pretty, 'tis a ripple,
Lapping, lapping, on the shore.
Mother watches, nought can harm you,
Angel warders gather nigh;
Blessed angels, bending o'er you,
Sing your lulla, lullaby.

BYE YOU, BYE YOU

Bye you, bye you, bye you, shikibye you,
Go to sleep my Glinka dear.
In the darkest trees of the forest,
All our feathered friends will sing,
As they work to build their nests
When at long last comes the spring.

Bye you, bye you, bye you, shikibye you,
Go to sleep my Glinka dear.
Nightingale, oh nightingale,
Do not weave yourself a nest,
Fly instead to our fine orchard,
There to dwell in happiness.

Bye you, bye you, bye you, shikibye you,
Go to sleep my Glinka dear.
Who will worry about your care?
Stay awake all through the night,
Who is it that loves you dearly?
Never lets you out of her sight.

Bye you, bye you, bye you, shikibye you,
Go to sleep my Glinka dear.
It is Mother, your dear Mother,
It's your precious Mother dear,
Who'll buy toys and tell you stories,
Shelter you from harm and fear.

TRADITIONAL RUSSIAN   131

HOPI LULLABY

Puva, puva, puva,
In the trail the beetles
On each other's backs are sleeping,
So on mine, my baby, thou.
Puva, puva, puva!

AKAN LULLABY

Someone would like to have you for her child
But you are mine.
Someone would like to rear you on a costly mat
But you are mine.
Someone would like to place you on a camel blanket
But you are mine.
I have you to rear on a torn old mat.
Someone would like to have you as her child
But you are mine.

LULLABY
(FOR A BLACK MOTHER)

My little dark baby,
My little earth-thing,
My little love-one,
What shall I sing
For your lullaby?

    Stars,
    Stars,
    A necklace of stars
    Winding the night.

My little black baby,
My dark body's baby,
What shall I sing
For your lullaby?

    Moon,
    Moon,
    Great diamond moon,
    Kissing the night.

Oh, little dark baby,
Night black baby,

    Stars, stars,
    Moon,
    Night stars,
    Moon,

For your sleep-song lullaby

LULLABY FOR A DAUGHTER

Someday, when the sands of time
invert, may you find perfect rest
as a newborn nurses from
the hourglass of your breast.

WHEN DADDY
COMES HOME

SWEET AND LOW

Sweet and low, sweet and low,
   Wind of the western sea,
Low, low, breathe and blow,
   Wind of the western sea!
Over the rolling waters go,
Come from the dying moon, and blow,
   Blow him again to me;
While my little one, while my pretty one, sleeps.

Sleep and rest, sleep and rest,
   Father will come to thee soon;
Rest, rest, on mother's breast,
   Father will come to thee soon;
Father will come to his babe in the nest,
Silver sails all out of the west
   Under the silver moon:
Sleep, my little one, sleep, my pretty one, sleep.

ALFRED, LORD TENNYSON (1809–92)

BYE, BABY BUNTING

Bye, baby bunting,
Daddy's gone a-hunting,
To get a little rabbit skin
To wrap his baby bunting in.

Bye, baby bunting,
Daddy's gone a-hunting,
To get a little lambie skin
To wrap his baby bunting in.

Bye, baby bunting,
Daddy's gone a-hunting,
A rosy wisp of cloud to win
To wrap his baby bunting in.

HUSH, MY BABY, DON'T YOU CRY

Hush, my baby, don't you cry,
Daddy's gonna come home by and by.
He will bring to his dear little baby
Candy and a kitty and a puppy dog maybe.
Hush, hush, hush and don't you cry,
Daddy's gonna come home by and by.

HUSH, LITTLE BABY,
DON'T SAY A WORD

Hush, little baby, don't say a word,
Papa's gonna buy you a mockingbird.

If that mockingbird don't sing,
Papa's gonna buy you a diamond ring.

If that diamond ring turns brass,
Papa's gonna buy you a looking glass.

If that looking glass gets broke,
Papa's gonna buy you a billy goat.

If that billy goat won't pull,
Papa's gonna buy you a cart and bull.

If that cart and bull turn over,
Papa's gonna buy you a dog named Rover.

If that dog named Rover won't bark,
Papa's gonna buy you a horse and cart.

If that horse and cart fall down,
You'll still be the sweetest little baby in town.

ALLY BALLY

Ally bally, ally bally bee,
Sittin' on your daddy's knee.
Wantin' for a wee penny
To buy some choc'late candy.

Ah, poor thing you're gettin' very thin,
A bundle of bones all covered with skin.
Now you're gettin' a wee double chin
From all that choc'late candy.

Go to sleep now, my little one,
Seven o'clock and your playing's done.
Open your eyes to the morning sun,
I'll give you some choc'late candy.

TRADITIONAL   143

WELSH LULLABY

A mother was pressing
Her babe to her breast,
And saying while soothing
His sorrow to rest:
"Sleep gently, my darling,
Sleep soundly, my boy,
For thou art my treasure,
My rapture and joy.
The trumpet is howling
Again and again,
Thy father is sailing
A-far on the main.
May Heav'n be his shield
On the deep heaving sea,
And bring him in safely
To thee and to me."

The lightning was vivid,
The thunder was loud,
The mother was praying,
And sobbing aloud.
Amid the wild moaning
Of nature in strife,
The captain sprang forward
And flew to his wife.

He kiss'd the fond mother,
He kiss'd his dear boy,
And gazed on them kindly,
Exclaiming with joy·
"I've made a good fortune,
And never will roam
Again from my wife,
My sweet child, and my home."

DANCE TO YOUR DADDY

Dance to your daddy,
My bonnie laddie,
Dance to your daddy,
My bonnie lamb.

You shall have a fishy,
In a little dishy,
You shall have a fishy
When the boat comes in.

You shall have a coatie,
And a pair of breekies,
And you'll get an eggy,
And a bit of ham.

You shall have a pony,
Fit to ride for ony,
And you'll get a whippy
For to make him gang.

Dance to your daddy,
My bonnie laddie,
Dance to your daddy,
My bonnie lamb.

SONG TO BE SUNG BY THE FATHER
OF INFANT FEMALE CHILDREN

My heart leaps up when I behold
A rainbow in the sky;
Contrariwise, my blood runs cold
When little boys go by.
For little boys as little boys,
No special hate I carry,
But now and then they grow to men,
And when they do, they marry.
No matter how they tarry,
Eventually they marry.
And, swine among the pearls,
They marry little girls.

Oh, somewhere, somewhere, an infant plays,
With parents who feed and clothe him.
Their lips are sticky with pride and praise,
But I have begun to loathe him.
Yes, I loathe with loathing shameless
This child who to me is nameless.
This bachelor child in his carriage
Gives never a thought to marriage,
But a person can hardly say knife
Before he will hunt him a wife.

I never see an infant (male),
A-sleeping in the sun,
Without I turn a trifle pale
And think is he the one?
Oh, first he'll want to crop his curls,
And then he'll want a pony,
And then he'll think of pretty girls,
And holy matrimony.
A cat without a mouse
Is he without a spouse.

Oh, somewhere he bubbles bubbles of milk,
And quietly sucks his thumbs.
His cheeks are roses painted on silk,
And his teeth are tucked in his gums.
But alas the teeth will begin to grow,
And the bubbles will cease to bubble;
Given a score of years or so,
The roses will turn to stubble.

He'll sell a bond, or he'll write a book,
And his eyes will get that acquisitive look,
And raging and ravenous for the kill,
He'll boldly ask for the hand of Jill.
This infant whose middle
Is diapered still
Will want to marry
My daughter Jill.

Oh sweet be his slumber and moist his middle!
My dreams, I fear, are infanticiddle.
A fig for embryo Lohengrins!
I'll open all his safety pins,
I'll pepper his powder, and salt his bottle,
And give him readings from Aristotle.
Sand for his spinach I'll gladly bring,
And Tabasco sauce for his teething ring.
Then perhaps he'll struggle through fire and water
To marry somebody else's daughter.

OGDEN NASH (1902–71)   149

WELCOME, STRANGER

BABY SONG

From the private ease of Mother's womb
I fall into the lighted room.

Why don't they simply put me back
Where it is warm and wet and black?

But one thing follows on another.
Things were different inside Mother.

Padded and jolly I would ride
The perfect comfort of her inside.

They tuck me in a rustling bed
— I lie there, raging, small, and red.

I may sleep soon, I may forget,
But I won't forget that I regret.

A rain of blood poured round her womb,
But all time roars outside this room.

MORNING SONG

Love set you going like a fat gold watch.
The midwife slapped your footsoles, and your bald cry
Took its place among the elements.

Our voices echo, magnifying your arrival. New statue.
In a drafty museum, your nakedness
Shadows our safety. We stand round blankly as walls.

I'm no more your mother
Than the cloud that distills a mirror to reflect its
        own slow
Effacement at the wind's hand.

All night your moth-breath
Flickers among the flat pink roses. I wake to listen:
A far sea moves in my ear.

One cry, and I stumble from bed, cow-heavy and floral
In my Victorian nightgown.
Your mouth opens clean as a cat's. The window square

Whitens and swallows its dull stars. And now you try
Your handful of notes;
The clear vowels rise like balloons.

WOMAN TO CHILD

You who were darkness warmed my flesh
where out of darkness rose the seed.
Then all a world I made in me;
all the world you hear and see
hung upon my dreaming blood.

There moved the multitudinous stars,
and coloured birds and fishes moved.
There swarm the sliding continents.
All time lay rolled in me, and sense,
and love that knew not its beloved.

O node and focus of the world;
I hold you deep within that well
you shall escape and not escape —
that mirrors still your sleeping shape;
that nurtures still your crescent cell.

I wither and you break from me;
yet though you dance in living light
I am the earth, I am the root,
I am the stem that fed the fruit,
the link that joins you to the night.

TO A TEN MONTHS' CHILD

Late arrival, no
One would think of blaming you
For hesitating so.

Who, setting his hand to knock
At a door so strange as this one,
Might not draw back?

Certainly, once admitted,
You will be made to feel
Like one of the invited.

Still, because you come
From so remote a kingdom,
You may feel out of place,

Tongue-tied and shy among
So many strangers, all
Babbling a strange tongue.

Well, that's no disgrace.
So might any person
So recently displaced,

Remembering the ocean,
So calm, so lately crossed.

AT BIRTH

Come from a distant country,
Bundle of flesh, of blood,
Demanding painful entry,
Expecting little good:
There is no going back
Among those thickets where
Both night and day are black
And blood's the same as air.

Strangely you come to meet us,
Stained, mottled, as if dead:
You bridge the dark hiatus
Through which your body slid
Across a span of muscle,
A breadth my hand can span.
The gorged and brimming vessel
Flows over, and is man.

Dear daughter, as I watched you
Come crumpled from the womb,
And sweating hands had fetched you
Into this world, the room
Opened before your coming
Like water struck from rocks
And echoed with your crying
Your living paradox.

ANTHONY THWAITE (1930–)   157

NOW THAT I AM
FOREVER WITH CHILD

How the days went
while you were blooming within me
I remember, each upon each
The swelling changed planes of my body
and how you first fluttered, then jumped
and I thought it was my heart.

How the days wound down
and the turning of winter
I recall, with you growing heavy
against the wind. I thought
now her hands are formed, and her hair
has started to curl
now her teeth are done
now she sneezes.
Then the seed opened.
I bore you one morning just before spring
My head rang like a fiery piston
my legs were towers between which
A new world was passing.

From then
I can only distinguish
one thread within running hours
You . . . flowing through selves
toward you.

POEMS FOR
CHILDREN

NONSENSE

TO BED

Come let's to bed,
    Says Sleepy-head;
Sit up a while, says Slow;
    Put on the pan
    Says Greedy Nan,
Let's sup before
    we go.

ANONYMOUS

HEY! DIDDLE, DIDDLE

Hey! diddle, diddle,
The cat and the fiddle,
The cow jumped over the moon;
The little dog laughed
To see such craft,
And the dish ran away with the spoon.

SING A SONG OF SIXPENCE

Sing a song of sixpence,
    Pockets full of rye;
Four and twenty blackbirds
    Baked in a pie.
When the pie was opened
    The birds began to sing;
Was not that a dainty dish
    To set before the king?

The king was in his counting-house
    Counting out his money;
The queen was in the parlour,
    Eating bread and honey;
The maid was in the garden
    Hanging out the clothes,
When down came a blackbird
    And pecked off her nose.

COMICAL FOLK

In a cottage in Fife
Lived a man and his wife,
Who, believe me, were comical folk;
For, to people's surprise,
They both saw with their eyes,
And their tongues moved whenever they spoke.

When they were asleep,
I'm told – that to keep
Their eyes open they could not contrive;
They both walked on their feet,
And 't was thought what they eat
Helped, with drinking, to keep them alive.

ANONYMOUS

THE CROOKED SONG

There was a crooked man,
    and he went a crooked mile,
He found a crooked sixpence
    beside a crooked stile;
He bought a crooked cat,
    which caught a crooked mouse,
And they all lived together
    in a little crooked house.

THE MAN IN THE WILDERNESS

The Man in the Wilderness asked of me
"How many blackberries grow in the sea?"
I answered him as I thought good,
"As many red herrings as grow in the wood."

The Man in the Wilderness asked me why
His hen could swim, and his pig could fly.
I answered him briskly as I thought best,
"Because they were born in a cuckoo's nest."

The Man in the Wilderness asked me to tell
The sands in the sea and I counted them well.
Says he with a grin, "And not one more?"
I answered him bravely, "You go and make sure."

ANONYMOUS   167

SELF-PORTRAIT OF EDWARD LEAR

How pleasant to know Mr Lear!
    Who has written such volumes of stuff!
Some think him ill-tempered and queer,
    But a few think him pleasant enough.

His mind is concrete and fastidious,
    His nose is remarkably big;
His visage is more or less hideous,
    His beard it resembles a wig.

He has ears, and two eyes, and ten fingers,
    Leastways if you reckon two thumbs;
Long ago he was one of the singers,
    But now he is one of the dumbs.

He sits in a beautiful parlour,
    With hundreds of books on the wall;
He drinks a great deal of marsala,
    But never gets tipsy at all.

He has many friends, laymen and clerical;
    Old Foss is the name of his cat;
His body is perfectly spherical,
    He weareth a runcible hat.

When he walks in a waterproof white,
    The children run after him so!
Calling out, "He's come out in his night-
    Gown, that crazy old Englishman, oh!"

He weeps by the side of the ocean,
    He weeps at the top of the hill;
He purchases pancakes and lotion,
    And chocolate shrimps from the mill.

He reads but he cannot speak Spanish,
    He cannot abide ginger-beer:
Ere the days of his pilgrimage vanish,
    How pleasant to know Mr Lear!

EDWARD LEAR (1812–88)   169

THE TABLE AND THE CHAIR

Said the Table to the Chair,
"You can hardly be aware,
How I suffer from the heat,
And from chilblains on my feet!
If we took a little walk,
We might have a little talk!
Pray let us take the air!"
Said the Table to the Chair.

Said the Chair unto the Table,
"Now you *know* we are not able!
How foolishly you talk,
When you know we *cannot* walk!"
Said the Table, with a sigh,
"It can do no harm to try,
I've as many legs as you,
Why can't we walk on two?"

So they both went slowly down,
And walked about the town
With a cheerful bumpy sound,
As they toddled round and round,
And everybody cried,
As they hastened to their side,
"See! the Table and the Chair
Have come out to take the air!"

But in going down an alley,
To a castle in a valley,
They completely lost their way,
And wandered all the day,
Till, to see them safely back,
They paid a Ducky-quack,
And a Beetle, and a Mouse,
Who took them to their house.

They whispered to each other,
"O delightful little brother!
What a lovely walk we've taken!
Let us dine on Beans and Bacon!"
So the Ducky, and the leetle
Browny-Mousy and the Beetle
Dined, and danced upon their heads
Till they toddled to their beds.

IF A PIG WORE A WIG

If a pig wore a wig,
   What could we say?
Treat him as a gentleman,
   And say "Good day."

If his tail chanced to fail,
   What could we do? –
Send him to the tailoress
   To get one new.

GROWING IN THE VALE

Growing in the vale
   By the uplands hilly,
Growing straight and frail,
   Lady Daffadowndilly,

In a golden crown,
And a scant green gown
   While the spring blows chilly,
Lady Daffadown,
   Sweet Daffadowndilly.

YOU ARE OLD, FATHER WILLIAM

"You are old, Father William," the young man said,
  "And your hair has become very white;
And yet you incessantly stand on your head –
  Do you think, at your age, it is right?"

"In my youth," Father William replied to his son,
  "I feared it might injure the brain;
But, now that I'm perfectly sure I have none,
  Why, I do it again and again."

"You are old," said the youth, "as I mentioned before,
  And have grown most uncommonly fat;
Yet you turned a back-somersault in at the door –
  Pray, what is the reason of that?"

"In my youth," said the sage, as he shook his grey locks,
  "I kept all my limbs very supple
By the use of this ointment – one shilling the box –
  Allow me to sell you a couple?"

"You are old," said the youth, "and your jaws are
    too weak
  For anything tougher than suet;
Yet you finished the goose, with the bones and
    the beak –
  Pray, how did you manage to do it?"

"In my youth," said his father, "I took to the law,
    And argued each case with my wife;
And the muscular strength, which it gave to my jaw,
    Has lasted the rest of my life."

"You are old," said the youth, "one would hardly suppose
    That your eye was as steady as ever,
Yet you balanced an eel on the end of your nose—
    What made you so awfully clever?"

"I have answered three questions, and that is enough,"
    Said his father. "Don't give yourself airs!
Do you think I can listen all day to such stuff?
    Be off, or I'll kick you downstairs!"

JABBERWOCKY

'Twas brillig, and the slithy toves
   Did gyre and gimble in the wabe:
All mimsy were the borogoves,
   And the mome raths outgrabe.

"Beware the Jabberwock, my son!
   The jaws that bite, the claws that catch!
Beware the Jubjub bird, and shun
   The frumious Bandersnatch!"

He took his vorpal sword in hand:
   Long time the manxome foe he sought –
So rested he by the Tumtum tree,
   And stood awhile in thought.

And as in uffish thought he stood,
   The Jabberwock, with eyes of flame,
Came whiffling through the tulgey wood,
   And burbled as it came!

One, two! One, two! And through and through
   The vorpal blade went snicker-snack!
He left it dead, and with its head
   He went galumphing back.

"And hast thou slain the Jabberwock?
    Come to my arms, my beamish boy!
O frabjous day! Callooh! Callay!"
    He chortled in his joy.

'Twas brillig, and the slithy toves
    Did gyre and gimble in the wabe:
All mimsy were the borogoves,
    And the mome raths outgrabe.

THE MOCK TURTLE'S SONG

"Will you walk a little faster," said a whiting to a snail,
"There's a porpoise close behind me, and he's treading
    on my tail.
See how eagerly the lobsters and the turtles all
    advance!
They are waiting on the shingle – will you come and
    join the dance?
    Will you, won't you, will you, won't you, will you
      join the dance?
    Will you, won't you, will you, won't you, won't you
      join the dance?"

"You can really have no notion how delightful it will be
When they take us up and throw us, with the lobsters,
    out to sea!"
But the snail replied "Too far, too far!" and gave a look
    askance –
Said he thanked the whiting kindly, but he would not
    join the dance.
    Would not, could not, would not, could not, would
      not join the dance.
    Would not, could not, would not, could not, could
      not join the dance.

"What matters it how far we go?" his scaly friend
    replied.
"There is another shore, you know, upon the other
    side.
The further off from England the nearer is to France —
Then turn not pale, beloved snail, but come and join
    the dance.
    Will you, won't you, will you, won't you, will you
        join the dance?
    Will you, won't you, will you, won't you, won't you
        join the dance?"

CRAQUEODOOM

The Crankadox leaned o'er the edge of the moon
    And wistfully gazed on the sea
Where the Gryxabodill madly whistled a tune
    To the air of "Ti-fol-de-ding-dee."
The quavering shriek of the Fly-up-the-creek
    Was fitfully wafted afar
To the Queen of the Wunks as she powdered her cheek
    With the pulverized rays of a star.

The Gool closed his ear on the voice of the Grig,
    And his heart it grew heavy as lead
As he marked the Baldekin adjusting his wig
    On the opposite side of his head,
And the air it grew chill as the Gryxabodill
    Raised his dank, dripping fins to the skies,
And plead with the Plunk for the use of her bill
    To pick the tears out of his eyes.

The ghost of the Zhack flitted by in a trance,
    And the Squidjum hid under a tub
As he heard the loud hooves of the Hooken advance
    With a rub-a-dub dub-a-dub dub!
And the Crankadox cried, as he laid down and died,
    "My fate there is none to bewail,"
While the Queen of the Wunks drifted over the tide
    With a long piece of crape to her tail.

180   JAMES WHITCOMB RILEY (1849–1916)

ELETELEPHONY

Once there was an elephant,
Who tried to use the telephant –
No! No! I mean an elephone
Who tried to use the telephone –
(Dear me! I am not certain quite
That even now I've got it right.)

Howe'er it was, he got his trunk
Entangled in the telephunk;
The more he tried to get it free,
The louder buzzed the telephee –
(I fear I'd better drop the song
Of elephop and telephong!)

LAURA E. RICHARDS (1850–1943)

SONG OF THE MAD PRINCE

Who said, "Peacock Pie"?
  The old King to the sparrow:
Who said, "Crops are ripe"?
  Rust to the harrow:
Who said, "Where sleeps she now?
  Where rests she now her head,
Bathed in eve's loveliness"? –
  That's what I said.

Who said, "Ay, mum's the word"?
  Sexton to willow:
Who said, "Green dusk for dreams.
  Moss for a pillow"?
Who said, "All Time's delight
  Hath she for narrow bed;
Life's troubled bubble broken"? –
  That's what I said.

ODE TO A BABY

A bit of talcum
Is always walcum.

SILLY STORIES

GOOD KING ARTHUR

When good King Arthur ruled this land
　　He was a goodly king;
He stole three pecks of barley-meal
　　To make a bag-pudding.

A bag-pudding the king did make,
　　And stuff'd it well with plums;
And in it put great lumps of fat,
　　As big as my two thumbs.

The king and queen did eat thereof,
　　And noble men beside;
And what they could not eat that night,
　　The queen next morning fried.

ANONYMOUS

THE QUEEN OF HEARTS

The Queen of Hearts she made some tarts,
    All on a summer's day;
The Knave of Hearts he stole those tarts,
    And took them clean away.

The King of Hearts called for those tarts,
    And beat the Knave full sore.
The Knave of Hearts brought back those tarts,
    And vowed he'd steal no more.

WEE WILLIE WINKIE

Wee Willie Winkie runs through the town,
Up stairs and down stairs, in his night-gown,
Rapping at the window, crying through the lock;
"Are the children in their beds, for it's past eight
    o'clock."

LITTLE BO-PEEP

Little Bo-Peep has lost her sheep,
    And can't tell where to find them;
Let them alone, and they'll come home,
    And bring their tails behind them.

Little Bo-Peep fell fast asleep,
    And dreamt she heard them bleating;
And when she awoke, she found it a joke,
    For still they were all fleeting.

Then up she took her little crook,
    Determined for to find them;
She found them indeed, but it made her heart bleed,
    For they'd left all their tails behind them.

It happened one day as Bo-Peep did stray
    Into a meadow hard by,
There she espied their tails side by side,
    All hung on a tree to dry.

She heaved a sigh, and wiped her eye,
    And went over hill and dale, oh;
And tried what she could, as a shepherdess should,
    To tack to each sheep its tail, oh!

AN ELEGY ON THE DEATH
OF A MAD DOG

Good people all, of every sort,
 Give ear unto my song;
And if you find it wond'rous short,
 It cannot hold you long.

In Islington there was a man,
 Of whom the world might say,
That still a godly race he ran,
 Whene'er he went to pray.

A kind and gentle heart he had,
 To comfort friends and foes;
The naked every day he clad,
 When he put on his clothes.

And in that town a dog was found,
 As many dogs there be,
Both mongrel, puppy, whelp and hound,
 And curs of low degree.

This dog and man at first were friends;
 But when a pique began,
The dog, to gain some private ends,
 Went mad and bit the man.

Around from all the neighbouring streets
　　The wondering neighbours ran,
And swore the dog had lost his wits,
　　To bite so good a man.

The wound it seemed both sore and sad
　　To every Christian eye;
And while they swore the dog was mad,
　　They swore the man would die.

But soon a wonder came to light,
　　That showed the rogues they lied:
The man recovered of the bite,
　　The dog it was that died.

THE COMIC ADVENTURES
OF OLD MOTHER HUBBARD
AND HER DOG

Old Mother Hubbard
Went to the cupboard,
To give the poor dog a bone;
When she came there
The cupboard was bare,
And so the poor dog had none.

She went to the baker's
To buy him some bread;
When she came back
The dog was dead.

She went to the undertaker's
To buy him a coffin;
When she came back
The dog was laughing.

She took a clean dish
To get him some tripe;
When she came back
He was smoking his pipe.

She went to the alehouse
    To get him some beer;
When she came back
    The dog sat in a chair.

She went to the tavern
    For white wine and red;
When she came back
    The dog stood on his head.

She went to the fruiterer's
    To buy him some fruit;
When she came back
    He was playing the flute.

She went to the tailor's
    To buy him a coat;
When she came back
    He was riding a goat.

She went to the hatter's
    To buy him a hat;
When she came back
    He was feeding the cat.

She went to the barber's
　　To buy him a wig;
When she came back
　　He was dancing a jig.

She went to the cobbler's
　　To buy him some shoes;
When she came back
　　He was reading the news.

She went to the seamstress
　　To buy him some linen;
When she came back
　　The dog was spinning.

She went to the hosier's
　　To buy him some hose;
When she came back
　　He was dressed in his clothes.

The dame made a curtsy,
　　The dog made a bow;
The dame said 'Your servant',
　　The dog said 'Bow-wow'.

SARAH CATHERINE MARTIN (1768–1826)　195

THE OWL AND THE PUSSY-CAT

The Owl and the Pussy-cat went to sea
    In a beautiful pea-green boat,
They took some honey, and plenty of money,
    Wrapped up in a five-pound note.
The Owl looked up to the stars above,
    And sang to a small guitar,
"O lovely Pussy! O Pussy, my love,
    What a beautiful Pussy you are,
        You are,
        You are!
    What a beautiful Pussy you are!"

Pussy said to the Owl, "You elegant fowl!
    How charmingly sweet you sing!
O let us be married! Too long we have tarried:
    But what shall we do for a ring?"
They sailed away, for a year and a day,
    To the land where the Bong-Tree grows,
And there in a wood a Piggy-wig stood,
    With a ring at the end of his nose,
        His nose,
        His nose,
    With a ring at the end of his nose.

"Dear Pig, are you willing to sell for one shilling
  Your ring?" Said the Piggy, "I will."
So they took it away, and were married next day
  By the Turkey who lives on the hill.
They dined on mince, and slices of quince,
  Which they ate with a runcible spoon;
And hand in hand, on the edge of the sand,
  They danced by the light of the moon,
        The moon,
        The moon,
  They danced by the light of the moon.

EDWARD LEAR (1812–88)

A TRAGIC STORY

There liv'd a sage in days of yore,
And he a handsome pigtail wore,
But wonder'd much and sorrow'd more,
Because it hung behind him.

He mus'd upon this curious case,
And swore he'd change the pigtail's place,
And have it dangling at his face,
Not dangling there behind him.

Says he, 'The mystery I've found, –
I'll turn me round." –
He turn'd him round,
But still it hung behind him.

Then round and round, and out and in,
All day the puzzled sage did spin;
In vain – it matter'd not a pin,
The pigtail hung behind him.

And right and left, and round about,
And up and down, and in and out he turn'd,
But still the pigtail stout
Hung steadily behind him.

And though his efforts never slack,
And though he twist, and twirl, and tack,
Alas! still faithful to his back,
The pigtail hangs behind him.

WHERE DID YOU COME FROM, BABY DEAR?

Where did you come from, baby dear?
Out of the everywhere into here.

Where did you get your eyes so blue?
Out of the sky as I came through.

What makes the light in them sparkle and spin?
Some of the starry spikes left in.

Where did you get that little tear?
I found it waiting when I got here.

What makes your forehead so smooth and high?
A soft hand stroked it as I went by.

What makes your cheek like a warm white rose?
I saw something better than anyone knows.

Whence that three-cornered smile of bliss?
Three angels gave me at once a kiss.

Where did you get this pearly ear?
God spoke, and it came out to hear.

Where did you get those arms and hands?
Love made itself into hooks and bands.

Feet, whence did you come, you darling things?
From the same box as the cherubs' wings.

How did they all just come to be you?
God thought about me, and so I grew.

But how did you come to us, you dear?
God thought about you, and so I am here.

GEORGE MacDONALD (1824–1905)

MOTHER SHAKE THE
CHERRY-TREE

Mother shake the cherry-tree,
   Susan catch a cherry;
Oh how funny that will be,
   Let's be merry!

One for brother, one for sister,
   Two for mother more,
Six for father, hot and tired,
   Knocking at the door.

THE WALRUS AND THE CARPENTER

The sun was shining on the sea,
    Shining with all his might:
He did his very best to make
    The billows smooth and bright –
And this was odd, because it was
    The middle of the night.

The moon was shining sulkily,
    Because she thought the sun
Had got no business to be there
    After the day was done –
"It's very rude of him," she said,
    "To come and spoil the fun!"

The sea was wet as wet could be,
    The sands were dry as dry.
You could not see a cloud, because
    No cloud was in the sky:
No birds were flying overhead –
    There were no birds to fly.

The Walrus and the Carpenter
    Were walking close at hand;
They wept like anything to see
    Such quantities of sand:
"If this were only cleared away,"
    They said, "it *would* be grand!"

"If seven maids with seven mops
  Swept it for half a year,
Do you suppose," the Walrus said,
  "That they could get it clear?"
"I doubt it," said the Carpenter,
  And shed a bitter tear.

"O Oysters, come and walk with us!"
  The Walrus did beseech.
"A pleasant walk, a pleasant talk,
  Along the briny beach:
We cannot do with more than four,
  To give a hand to each."

The eldest Oyster looked at him,
  But never a word he said:
The eldest Oyster winked his eye,
  And shook his heavy head –
Meaning to say he did not choose
  To leave the oyster-bed.

But four young Oysters hurried up,
  All eager for the treat:
Their coats were brushed, their faces washed,
  Their shoes were clean and neat –
And this was odd, because, you know,
  They hadn't any feet.

Four other Oysters followed them,
And yet another four;
And thick and fast they came at last,
And more, and more, and more –
All hopping through the frothy waves,
And scrambling to the shore.

The Walrus and the Carpenter
Walked on a mile or so,
And then they rested on a rock
Conveniently low:
And all the little Oysters stood
And waited in a row.

"The time has come," the Walrus said,
"To talk of many things:
Of shoes – and ships – and sealing wax –
Of cabbages – and kings –
And why the sea is boiling hot –
And whether pigs have wings."

"But wait a bit," the Oysters cried,
"Before we have our chat;
For some of us are out of breath,
And all of us are fat!"
"No hurry!" said the Carpenter.
They thanked him much for that.

"A loaf of bread," the Walrus said,
    "Is what we chiefly need:
Pepper and vinegar besides
    Are very good indeed –
Now if you're ready, Oysters dear,
    We can begin to feed."

"But not on us!" the Oysters cried,
    Turning a little blue,
"After such kindness, that would be
    A dismal thing to do!"
"The night is fine," the Walrus said.
    "Do you admire the view?

"It was so kind of you to come!
    And you are very nice!"
The Carpenter said nothing but
    "Cut us another slice:
I wish you were not quite so deaf –
    I've had to ask you twice!"

"It seems a shame," the Walrus said,
    "To play them such a trick,
After we've brought them out so far,
    And made them trot so quick!"
The Carpenter said nothing but
    "The butter's spread too thick!"

"I weep for you," the Walrus said,
  "I deeply sympathize."
With sobs and tears he sorted out
  Those of the largest size,
Holding his pocket-handkerchief
  Before his streaming eyes.

"O Oysters," said the Carpenter,
  "You've had a pleasant run!
Shall we be trotting home again?"
  But answer came there none –
And this was scarcely odd, because
  They'd eaten every one.

BED IN SUMMER

In winter I get up at night
And dress by yellow candle-light.
In summer, quite the other way,
I have to go to bed by day.

I have to go to bed and see
The birds still hopping on the tree,
Or hear the grown-up people's feet
Still going past me in the street.

And does it not seem hard to you,
When all the sky is clear and blue,
And I should like so much to play,
To have to go to bed by day?

MY SHADOW

I have a little shadow that goes in and out with me,
And what can be the use of him is more than I can see.
He is very, very like me from the heels up to the head;
And I see him jump before me, when I jump into my bed.

The funniest thing about him is the way he likes
      to grow —
Not at all like proper children, which is always
      very slow;
For he sometimes shoots up taller like an India-
      rubber ball,
And he sometimes gets so little that there's none
      of him at all.

He hasn't got a notion of how children ought to play,
And can only make a fool of me in every sort of way.
He stays so close beside me, he's a coward you can see;
I'd think shame to stick to nursie as that shadow sticks
      to me!

One morning, very early, before the sun was up,
I rose and found the shining dew on every buttercup;
But my lazy little shadow, like an arrant sleepy-head,
Had stayed at home behind me and was fast asleep
      in bed.

ROBERT LOUIS STEVENSON (1850–94)   209

THE TALE OF CUSTARD THE DRAGON

Belinda lived in a little white house,
With a little black kitten and a little gray mouse,
And a little yellow dog and a little red wagon,
And a realio, trulio, little pet dragon.

Now the name of the little black kitten was Ink,
And the little gray mouse, she called him Blink,
And the little yellow dog was sharp as Mustard,
But the dragon was a coward, and she called him
       Custard.

Custard the dragon had big sharp teeth,
And spikes on top of him and scales underneath,
Mouth like a fireplace, chimney for a nose,
And realio, trulio daggers on his toes.

Belinda was as brave as a barrel full of bears,
And Ink and Blink chased lions down the stairs,
Mustard was as brave as a tiger in a rage,
But Custard cried for a nice safe cage.

Belinda tickled him, she tickled him unmerciful,
Ink, Blink and Mustard, they rudely called him
       Percival,
They all sat laughing in the little red wagon
At the realio, trulio, cowardly dragon.

Belinda giggled till she shook the house,
And Blink said Weeck! which is giggling for a mouse,
Ink and Mustard rudely asked his age,
When Custard cried for a nice safe cage.

Suddenly, suddenly they heard a nasty sound,
And Mustard growled, and they all looked around.
Meowch! cried Ink, and Ooh! cried Belinda,
For there was a pirate, climbing in the winda.

Pistol in his left hand, pistol in his right,
And he held in his teeth a cutlass bright,
His beard was black, one leg was wood;
It was clear that the pirate meant no good.

Belinda paled, and she cried Help! Help!
But Mustard fled with a terrified yelp,
Ink trickled down to the bottom of the household,
And little mouse Blink strategically mouseholed.

But up jumped Custard snorting like an engine,
Clashed his tail like irons in a dungeon,
With a clatter and a clank and a jangling squirm,
He went at the pirate like a robin at a worm.

The pirate gaped at Belinda's dragon,
And gulped some grog from his pocket flagon,
He fired two bullets, but they didn't hit,
And Custard gobbled him, every bit.

Belinda embraced him, Mustard licked him,
No one mourned for his pirate victim.
Ink and Blink in glee did gyrate
Around the dragon that ate the pirate.

But presently up spoke little dog Mustard,
I'd been twice as brave if I hadn't been flustered.
And up spoke Ink and up spoke Blink,
We'd have been three times as brave, we think.
And Custard said, I quite agree
That everybody is braver than me.

Belinda still lives in her little white house,
With her little black kitten and her little gray mouse,
And her little yellow dog and her little red wagon,
And her realio, trulio, little pet dragon.

Belinda is as brave as a barrel full of bears,
And Ink and Blink chase lions down the stairs,
Mustard is as brave as a tiger in a rage,
But Custard keeps crying for a nice safe cage.

FANTASIES

I SAW A SHIP A SAILING

I saw a ship a-sailing,
    A-sailing on the sea;
And it was full of pretty things
    For baby and for me.

There were sweetmeats in the cabin,
    And apples in the hold;
The sails were made of silk,
    And the masts were made of gold.

The four-and-twenty sailors
    That stood between the decks,
Were four-and-twenty white mice,
    With chains about their necks.

The captain was a duck,
    With a packet on his back,
And when the ship began to move,
    The captain cried, "Quack, quack!"

KING PIPPIN'S HALL

King Pippin built a fine new hall,
Pastry and pie-crust were the wall;
Windows made of black pudding and white,
Slates were pancakes, you ne'er saw the like.

ANONYMOUS

IF

If all the world were apple-pie,
   And all the water ink,
What should we do for bread and cheese?
   What should we do for drink?

LAUGHING SONG

When the green woods laugh with the voice of joy,
And the dimpling stream runs laughing by;
When the air does laugh with our merry wit,
And the green hill laughs with the noise of it;

When the meadows laugh with lively green,
And the grasshopper laughs in the merry scene;
When Mary and Susan and Emily
With their sweet round mouths sing 'Ha, ha, he!'

When the painted birds laugh in the shade,
When our table with cherries and nuts is spread:
Come live, and be merry, and join with me
To sing the sweet chorus of 'Ha, ha, he!'

WILLIAM BLAKE (1757–1827)

THE SPLENDOUR FALLS ON
CASTLE WALLS
From *The Princess*

The splendour falls on castle walls
    And snowy summits old in story:
The long light shakes across the lakes,
    And the wild cataract leaps in glory.
Blow, bugle, blow, set the wild echoes flying,
Blow, bugle; answer, echoes, dying, dying, dying.

O hark, O hear! How thin and clear,
    And thinner, clearer, farther going!
O sweet and far from cliff and scar
    The horns of Elfland faintly blowing!
Blow, let us hear the purple glens replying:
Blow, bugle; answer, echoes, dying, dying, dying.

O love, they die in yon rich sky,
    They faint on hill or field or river;
Our echoes roll from soul to soul,
    And grow for ever and for ever.
Blow, bugle, blow, set the wild echoes flying,
And answer, echoes, answer, dying, dying, dying.

THE SUGAR-PLUM TREE

Have you ever heard of the Sugar-Plum Tree?
   'Tis a marvel of great renown!
It blooms on the shore of the Lollipop sea
   In the garden of Shut-Eye Town;
The fruit that it bears is so wondrously sweet
   (As those who have tasted it say)
That good little children have only to eat
   Of that fruit to be happy next day

When you've got to the tree, you would have
    a hard time
   To capture the fruit which I sing;
The tree is so tall that no person could climb
   To the boughs where the sugar-plums swing.
But up in that tree sits a chocolate cat,
   And a gingerbread dog prowls below —
And this is the way you contrive to get at
   Those sugar-plums tempting you so:

You say but the word to that gingerbread dog
   And he barks with such terrible zest
That the chocolate cat is at once all agog,
   As her swelling proportions attest.
And the chocolate cat goes cavorting around
   From this leafy limb unto that,

And the sugar-plums tumble, of course, to the
      ground –
  Hurrah for that chocolate cat!

There are marshmallows, gumdrops, and
      peppermint canes,
  With stripings of scarlet or gold,
And you carry away of the treasure that rains
  As much as your apron can hold!
So come, little child, cuddle closer to me
  In your dainty white nightcap and gown,
And I'll rock you away to that Sugar-Plum Tree
  In the garden of Shut-Eye Town.

YOUNG NIGHT THOUGHT

All night long, and every night,
When my mamma puts out the light,
I see the people marching by,
As plain as day, before my eye.

Armies and emperors and kings,
All carrying different kinds of things,
And marching in so grand a way,
You never saw the like by day.

So fine a show was never seen
At the great circus on the green;
For every kind of beast and man
Is marching in that caravan.

At first they move a little slow,
But still the faster on they go.
And still beside them close I keep
Until we reach the town of Sleep.

ROBERT LOUIS STEVENSON (1850–94)   221

THE LAND OF COUNTERPANE

When I was sick and lay a-bed,
I had two pillows at my head,
And all my toys beside me lay
To keep me happy all the day.

And sometimes for an hour or so
I watched my leaden soldiers go,
With different uniforms and drills,
Among the bedclothes, through the hills;

And sometimes sent my ships in fleets
All up and down among the sheets;
Or brought my trees and houses out,
And planted cities all about.

I was the giant great and still
That sits upon the pillow-hill,
And sees before him, dale and plain,
The pleasant land of counterpane.

ANIMALS

BAT, BAT

Bat, bat,
Come under my hat,
And I'll give you a slice of bacon;
And when I bake,
I'll give you a cake,
If I am not mistaken.

BOW-WOW, SAYS THE DOG

Bow-wow, says the dog;
　　Mew-mew, says the cat;
Grunt, grunt, goes the hog;
　　And squeak, goes the rat.

Chirp, chirp, says the sparrow;
　　Caw, caw, says the crow;
Quack, quack, says the duck;
　　And what cuckoos say, you know.

So, with sparrows and cuckoos,
　　With rats and with dogs,
With ducks and with crows,
　　With cats and with hogs,

A fine song I have made,
　　To please you, my dear;
And if it's well sung,
　　'Twill be charming to hear.

THE QUARRELSOME KITTENS

Two little kittens one stormy night,
They began to quarrel and they began to fight;
One had a mouse and the other had none,
And that's the way the quarrel begun.

"I'll have that mouse," said the bigger cat.
"You'll have that mouse? we'll see about that!"
"I will have that mouse," said the eldest son.
"You sha'n't have the mouse," said the little one.

I told you before 'twas a stormy night
When these two little kittens began to fight;
The old woman seized her sweeping broom,
And swept the two kittens right out of the room.

The ground was covered with frost and snow,
And the two little kittens had nowhere to go;
So they laid them down on the mat at the door,
While the old woman finished sweeping the floor.

Then they crept in, as quiet as mice,
All wet with the snow, and as cold as ice,
For they found it was better, that stormy night,
To lie down and sleep than to quarrel and fight.

ANONYMOUS   227

TO MARKET

To market, to market,
    To buy a fat pig;
Home again, home again,
    Jiggety jig.

To market, to market,
    To buy a fat hog;
Home again, home again,
    Jiggety jog.

ANONYMOUS

DICKERY, DICKERY, DARE

Dickery, dickery, dare,
The pig flew up in the air;
The man in brown soon brought him down,
Dickery, dickery, dare.

A GUINEA-PIG SONG

There was a little guinea-pig,
Who, being little, was not big;
He always walked upon his feet,
And never fasted when he eat.

When from a place he run away,
He never at the place did stay;
And while he run, as I am told,
He ne'er stood still for young or old.

He often squeaked, and sometimes violent,
And when he squeaked he ne'er was silent.
Though ne'er instructed by a cat,
He knew a mouse was not a rat.

One day, as I am certified,
He took a whim and fairly died;
And as I am told by men of sense,
He never has been living since.

ANONYMOUS (1773)   229

SPRING

Sound the Flute!
Now it's mute.
Birds delight
Day and Night;
Nightingale
In the dale,
Lake in Sky,
Merrily,
Merrily, Merrily to welcome in the Year.

Little Boy
Full of joy;
Little Girl,
Sweet and small,
Cock does crow,
So do you;
Merry voice,
Infant noise,
Merrily, Merrily to welcome in the Year.

Little Lamb,
Here I am;
Come and lick
My white neck;
Let me pull
Your soft Wool,
Let me kiss
Your soft face:
Merrily, Merrily, we welcome in the Year.

THE TYGER

Tyger! Tyger! burning bright
In the forests of the night,
What immortal hand or eye,
Did frame thy fearful symmetry?

In what distant deeps or skies
Burnt the fire of thine eyes?
On what wings dare he aspire?
What the hand dare seize the fire?

And what shoulder, and what art,
Could twist the sinews of thy heart?
And, when thy heart began to beat,
What dread hand? and what dread feet?

What the hammer? what the chain?
In what furnace was thy brain?
What the anvil? what dread grasp
Dare its deadly terrors clasp?

When the stars threw down their spears,
And water'd heaven with their tears,
Did he smile his work to see?
Did he who made the Lamb make thee?

Tyger! Tyger! burning bright
In the forests of the night,
What immortal hand or eye,
Did frame thy fearful symmetry?

THE LAMB

Little lamb, who made thee?
Dost thou know who made thee?
Gave thee life, and bid thee feed
By the stream and o'er the mead;
Gave thee clothing of delight,
Softest clothing, woolly, bright;
Gave thee such a tender voice,
Making all the vales rejoice?
Little lamb, who made thee?
Dost thou know who made thee?

Little lamb, I'll tell thee,
Little lamb, I'll tell thee:
He is callèd by thy name,
For he calls himself a lamb.
He is meek, and he is mild;
He became a little child.
I a child, and thou a lamb,
We are callèd by his name.
Little lamb, God bless thee!
Little lamb, God bless thee!

ANSWER TO A CHILD'S QUESTION

Do you ask what the birds say? The sparrow, the dove,
The linnet and thrush say, 'I love and I love!'
In the winter they're silent — the wind is so strong;
What it says, I don't know, but it sings a loud song.
But green leaves, and blossoms, and sunny warm
　　　weather,
And singing, and loving — all come back together.
But the lark is so brimful of gladness and love,
The green fields below him, the blue sky above,
That he sings, and he sings, and for ever sings he —
'I love my Love, and my Love loves me!'

SAMUEL TAYLOR COLERIDGE (1772–1834)　　235

HOW DOTH THE LITTLE CROCODILE

How doth the little crocodile
    Improve his shining tail,
And pour the waters of the Nile
    On every golden scale!

How cheerfully he seems to grin,
    How neatly spreads his claws,
And welcomes little fishes in
    With gently smiling jaws!

BEE! I'M EXPECTING YOU!

Bee! I'm expecting you!
Was saying Yesterday
To Somebody you know
That you were due —

The Frogs got Home last Week —
Are settled, and at work —
Birds, mostly back —
The Clover warm and thick —

You'll get my Letter by
The seventeenth; Reply
Or better, be with me —
Yours, Fly.

EMILY DICKINSON (1830-86)   237

THE FROG

Be kind and tender to the Frog,
  And do not call him names,
As "Slimy skin", or "Polly-wog",
  Or likewise "Ugly James",
Or "Gap-a-grin", or "Toad-gone wrong",
  Or "Bill Bandy-knees":
The Frog is justly sensitive
  To epithets like these.
No animal will more repay
  A treatment kind and fair;
At least so lonely people say
Who keep a frog (and, by the way,
  They are extremely rare).

HILAIRE BELLOC (1870–1953)

THE NAMING OF CATS

The Naming of Cats is a difficult matter,
    It isn't just one of your holiday games;
You may think at first I'm as mad as a hatter
When I tell you, a cat must have THREE
        DIFFERENT NAMES.
First of all, there's the name that the family use daily,
    Such as Peter, Augustus, Alonzo or James,
Such as Victor or Jonathan, George or Bill Bailey —
All of them sensible everyday names.
There are fancier names if you think they sound
        sweeter.
    Some for the gentlemen, some for the dames:
Such as Plato, Admetus, Electra, Demeter —
But all of them sensible everyday names.
But I tell you, a cat needs a name that's particular,
    A name that's peculiar, and more dignified,
Else how can he keep up his tail perpendicular,
    Or spread out his whiskers, or cherish his pride?
Of names of this kind, I can give you a quorum,
    Such as Munkustrap, Quaxo, or Coricopat,
Such as Bombalurina, or else Jellylorum —
Names that never belong to more than one cat.
But above and beyond there's still one name left over,
And that is the name that you never will guess;
The name that no human research can discover —

But THE CAT HIMSELF KNOWS, and will
    never confess.
When you notice a cat in profound meditation,
    The reason, I tell you, is always the same:
His mind is engaged in a rapt contemplation
    Of the thought, of the thought, of the thought
        of his name:
                His ineffable effable
                Effinineffable
Deep and inscrutable singular Name.

THE SONG OF THE JELLICLES

Jellicle Cats come out tonight
Jellicle Cats come one come all:
The Jellicle Moon is shining bright –
Jellicles come to the Jellicle Ball.

Jellicle Cats are black and white,
Jellicle Cats are rather small;
Jellicle Cats are merry and bright,
And pleasant to hear when they caterwaul.
Jellicle Cats have cheerful faces,
Jellicle Cats have bright black eyes;
They like to practise their airs and graces
And wait for the Jellicle Moon to rise.

Jellicle Cats develop slowly,
Jellicle Cats are not too big;
Jellicle Cats are roly-poly,
They know how to dance a gavotte and a jig.
Until the Jellicle Moon appears
They make their toilette and take their repose:
Jellicles wash behind their ears,
Jellicles dry between their toes.

Jellicle Cats are white and black,
Jellicle Cats are of moderate size;
Jellicles jump like a jumping-jack,
Jellicle Cats have moonlit eyes.
They're quiet enough in the morning hours,
They're quiet enough in the afternoon,
Reserving their terpsichorean powers
To dance by the light of the Jellicle Moon.

Jellicle Cats are black and white,
Jellicle Cats (as I said) are small;
If it happens to be a stormy night
They will practise a caper or two in the hall.
If it happens the sun is shining bright
You would say they had nothing to do at all:
They are resting and saving themselves to
        be right
For the Jellicle Moon and the Jellicle Ball.

THE OPOSSUM'S DREAM

Opossum
I hang from
the limb

of sleep,
hip to thigh
and thigh to

knee, and in
my dream
become a

leaf, tail to
sprout and skin
to green, a

leaf holding
fast to the
big tree, twig

to turn and
breeze to free.
Then stem to

breath and bud
to sleek, I
feel myself

in my night
dream, rib to
fin and gill

to breathe,
become a
trout, swimming

downstream fast
to the wide
sea, scale to

flash, grass to
weed, and at
the river's mouth

I feel, fresh
to salt and
mute to bark,

the trout I
am become
a seal, gliding

slow and warm,
deep beneath,
who bobs her

head up to
inquire, *Is
it morning?*

– But no,
the stars
are fired –

and diving
down becomes
a whale, dark

and huge, a world
entire –
seas and farms,

towns and fields,
breathing deep
until I feel

the sleep I'm
sleeping is
a bear's, who

curling in
his shambled
dream, fur

to wing and
tooth to beak,
dreams himself

small and
is a bird –
a bird who

stirs and sings:
I am a boy
asleep

in the green
tree's arms . . .
Opossum

I hang from
the limb
of sleep.

ACKNOWLEDGMENTS

Thanks are due to the following copyright holders for their permission to reprint:

'Akan Lullaby' translated by Professor Kwabena Nketia. From *African Poetry*, edited by Ulli Beier, published by Cambridge University Press. Copyright © Professor Kwabena Nketia. ANDERSEN, HANS CHRISTIAN: 'Mother and Child' by Hans Christian Andersen, translated by Inger Nielsen. 'Bye You, Bye You' from *Folk Lullabies of the World*, edited by Kenneth Peacock, published by Oak Publications, a division of Music Sales Corporation. DICKINSON, EMILY: 'Bee! I'm Expecting You!', reprinted by permission of the publishers and the Trustees of Amherst College from *The Poems of Emily Dickinson*, Thomas H. Johnson, ed., Cambridge, Mass.: The Belknap Press of Harvard University Press, Copyright © 1951, 1955, 1979 by the President and Fellows of Harvard College. BELLOC, HILAIRE: 'The Frog' from *Complete Verse* by Hilaire Belloc. Reprinted by permission of PFD on behalf of: The Estate of Hilaire Belloc. Copyright © The Estate of Hilaire Belloc 1970. DE LA MARE, WALTER: 'Song of The Mad Prince' from *The Complete Poems of Walter de la Mare* by Walter de la Mare. Reprinted by permission of The Literary Trustees of Walter de la Mare and the Society of Authors as their representative. ELIOT, T. S.: 'The Naming of the Cats' and 'The Song of the Jellicles' from *Old Possum's Book of Practical Cats* by T. S. Eliot. Reprinted by permission of Faber and Faber Ltd. in the UK. In the US: Copyright © 1939 by T. S. Eliot and renewed 1967 by Esme Valerie Eliot, reprinted by permission of Harcourt, Inc. GERSHWIN: 'Summertime' from *Porgy and Bess* by George Gershwin, DuBose and

247

INDEX OF FIRST LINES

252

254